MY LIFE

JOURNEY OF AN EMPLOYEE

RAJNEESH GUPTA

This book is dedicated to millions of employees toiling through day and night to achieve their dreams in their professional lives.

Contents

Foreword

This book is an inspiration for all, especially young managers and executives striving to find happiness and success in their jobs

Acknowledgements

I acknowledge my wife Ranjana Gupta who motivated me to share my rich professional experience with others in the form of a book. I also acknowledge my bosses, peers and team members for giving me golden moments

CHAPTER ONE

From student to professional

It was a pleasant June early morning when I entered the professional world of industry, machines, ranks and bosses. I was in for a shock because now I cannot bunk classes, sleep to my heart's content and worst from being senior most in engineering college I was the junior most in staff as a trainee.

College routine – Get up as you please, get ready, wear whatever you want to, attend the class, return to hostel, and then slog out at games and tracks, take dinner and sleep.

Factory routine – Get up at 5AM, get dressed in company uniform, catch the bus at 6.30 and after that the whole day is a blur, sit in the bus at 6PM and go to sleep before it crosses the company gates, reach home at 9PM, dinner and sleep and then the next day and the next and so on. God how I used to wait for Sundays.

The true lessons started when I missed the lunch because of pending task, getting hauled up for not finishing the task on time, being rebuked when I took a nap at my desk after a hard day's work, getting complaints that I do not wish my seniors and many more.

So a soft bellied boy started to get disciplined in life. Thanks to my boss and mentor at work I quickly learned the lessons which were the foundation stone for rest of my career spanning 37 years.

CHAPTER TWO

Life Altering Philosophies

After initial hiccups, I settled down as maintenance engineer and realised that to enjoy my work, I must adopt philosophies altering my life.

First one- Know your subject in detail and then attempt the task

Second one- Do not stop asking questions for the fear of being labelled as 'Stupid'

Third one- Learn from anyone and all the time. My best teachers were my electricians and mechanics.

Fourth one- Do not hesitate to make mistakes but learn from them and do not repeat them

Fifth one- Have dignity of labour

? One day there was unusual absenteeism and the Utility machines needed cleaning and oiling. I put on the overalls over my company uniform, took oil pump and cleaning dusters. For full day, I cleaned and oiled the machines. What do you think was my respect level with my subordinates the next day!!!!

? One instant I still remember. I was to check the voltage of a panel. By mistake I set the multimeter knob to Resistance instead of Voltage and went ahead. The multimeter just blasted out of my hand. Till today if I have to operate any equipment even in my house, I make sure that settings are correct.

? In another incident I changed over the electric supply from State Electricity Board to our own DG sets for running of Plant. I did not realise that the changeover switch was faulty. There was panic all around because our DG sets were charging the State Electricity Board power lines now. Someone could have had fatal accident that day but since my intentions were pure, so the invisible hand of GOD protected us all.

So learn, learn and keep on learning

Result - ? I was confirmed from trainee to Executive level in 9 months Instead of mandated 12 months.

Can you imagine the sense of achievement I got and that too in a salary of Rs1800/- per month. The savings from salary enabled to buy my first motorcycle 2 years later.

CHAPTER THREE

The Luck Smiles Down

I was happy in my job. Then, there was turn of eveThe Luck Smiles Downnnts, which would decide the exponential growth of my professional career.

One of my colleagues, had left the current company and joined an Indo-Japanese green field project. The Japanese company was a big name in engineering and household products world-wide, known for its quality. He took my resume and submitted it to the HR of new company for placement in Maintenance department.

Soon I got a call for interview. The interview panel consisted of 7 interviewers hailing from IIT Delhi and senior most persons of the company. Obviously, the interview was tough. But since I was truthful and honest about my experience (without adding any flair to it), I sailed through.

Then I forgot all about it in the rush of routine of my present duties. Imagine my surprise when I got the appointment letter from new company. And lo and behold, my happiness knew no bounds when I realised that I have been selected for Production department. And the icing on the cake was that I must submit my passport because I was to stay in Japan for a substantial period of time to learn and transfer the technology from Japan to India. In those days going abroad to a developed country was the domain of rich and famous. I thanked my stars.

I was to take-off in 20 days. Then came the obstacle because my present company was not ready to let me go. I was nervous as hell because it was once in a lifetime opportunity for a young man of 23. I pleaded with all the bosses and concerned seniors including the head of plant for early relieving, but they were adamant. I do not blame them because notice period was of 30 days.

Again, the luck smiled down. I came to know that a distant uncle was at a senior position in Corporate HR of current company. In those days emails did not exist. One letter from my uncle to the Plant Head changed the scene. Everyone was so surprised that I had an uncle at a position of high priest and never once I took advantage of his position. All the seniors adored me for this integrity, and I was relieved well in time from my present duties to join a new world.

Learning - Do your best and be honest to your commitments, rest assured the invisible power will take care of you.

The question remained as to how my resume went from Maintenance to Production file. Later on, I came to know that Japanese wanted one Electrical Engineer in the whole Production group to handle Laser based technology not yet available in India. So, the Interview Panel decided that I was the right choice.

Hence the destiny smiled and played her cards in my favour.

That's all folks. More on the Japanese way in next chapter.

CHAPTER FOUR

To the Land of Rising Sun

In April 1987, I walked into my new job with Passport in hand and dreams in the eyes. The site was under construction, so we were stationed at Corporate Office and waited for our flying day which was 17th May 1987.

Meanwhile, I utilised the time by going through technology know-how and learnt Japanese common words and their counting (which came really handy later). Also learnt how to behave in Japan, their history and culture.

Finally, the day arrived, and we all reached the Palam Airport. Since it was my first time to fly in airplane, I was nervous. Adding to that my whole maternal family arrived with garlands and aarti ??. I was flabbergasted.

Well, we settled down and got accustomed to the interiors of aircraft. I had heard a lot about smart airhostesses but all I saw was bodybuilders in the uniforms of flight attendants. The refreshments were served in a manner that if we question about choice of meals, they will take away the served portion also. And the looks they gave us said that do not dare to press the call button ?. Well, that was my first experience with Alitalia.

Finally, we reached Narita airport near Tokyo after change of planes at Hong Kong. Cathey Pacific service was right opposite of Alitalia. There was a reception committee waiting to receive us. And transport us to our first destination Fukaya.

My first impression and lasting impression of Japan was:

-No sound (No honking and useless chatter)

-No littering and dust (The places were spic and span)

-The humility of Japanese (Their politeness and hospitability- they will bow from waist at each greeting, suggestion and introduction)

-Extremely health conscious (Fit to the core with no bear belly to show)

-Punctuality (They stick to their schedules and complete everything on time)

-Discipline (Traffic, lines, their movements- almost everything)

-Vending machines for almost everything (I had never seen one before)- Because of low population the manual labour is very costly hence they try to robotise everything.

Late in the night we reached our hotel and prepared for a good night sleep after a long day of travel

------more on Japanese in next chapter.

CHAPTER FIVE

Experiences and Learnings in Japan

Next day, after reaching Fukaya, there was an introduction meeting at 8AM. It is a business code for Japanese to reach 5 minutes prior to any scheduled meeting or function. This was true then and this is true now. Even in India, they do not give excuses of traffic or rains and never reach late. I realised that for every activity, big or small, they plan meticulously. There is a saying in Japan that "instead of cutting a tree with blunt axe for 8 hours, sharpen it for 2 hours and cut it in 2 hours". That's the secret of their efficient and exponential rise after world war 2 to become one of the best countries in the world.

After introduction round, the team was split into two and our team accompanied our trainers to go to Taishi-Cho, a quaint little town, some 500 kms from Tokyo. The excitement was high when we boarded the iconic Bullet Train for the travel. At that time it was the fastest train in the world with a speed of 320km/hr (Now it is 600km/hr).. The comfort, smoothness and service was compared to nothing what we had experienced so far.

Taishi is a beautiful place, lush green with the view of snow-capped mountains in Himeji far away. The population consisted of 3000 employees of factory and farming community. We were told that no foreigner has stepped in Taishi for last 100 years. So, it came as no surprise when everyone walking or riding or driving stopped and greeted us especially when one of our senior member was 6 feet plus tall ?.

The town had no dust and the weather was perfect, so much so that we use to wear the company uniforms from Monday to Friday and washed them on Saturdays. Later did I realise as to why only one set has been given to us. (Was introduced to washing machine then)

One day we got called to our trainer's office because he had received the complaint from City Sanitation department that we had not separated the garbage into different bags of paper, plastic and metal. We got our first lesson on seriousness of recycling and reusing the waste.

Exchange of gifts is a big tradition in Japan. Silk and tea from India is a big rage with them. In anticipation we had taken lots of them with us from India and gifted them to our neighbours and trainers. They were overwhelmed.

On day we were introduced to a Senior Manager tool room. Suddenly I recalled that I have seen this person cleaning the floor and tea tables for the whole week. We were told that all employees are required to keep their designated areas/machines/utilities neat and clean by rotation. That inculcates the culture of my company, my place and my machine. No wonder they take pride in their work and workplace and nation at large.

I did not possess a wristwatch at that time. I bought a simple one made by Sieko for 12000 Yen (10 Yen= 1 Rs at that time). The warranty card assured of performance with a probable error of plus minus 5 seconds in a year. I still wear that watch and in 35 years it has not slipped by even 1 second. That's the real meaning of living and breathing quality. Japanese customer centricity in giving perfection to their products and services has taken them far and beyond.

CHAPTER SIX

Yet some more from Japan

Punctuality

Japan, as a country, is fanatic about punctuality. Whenever we took bus or train to travel, they were spot on time as per the written schedule. So, the travellers can plan their itinerary in advance.

I remember one incidence. Our factory was across the road to our residence. We used to walk to the road and wait for light to turn green for pedestrians. I noticed that our neighbour used to come and did not wait. The light would turn green as soon as she reached the zebra crossing. I asked her how. She explained that every day the light turns green at 7.49AM, so she plans her walk in a manner that she doesn't have ro wait. Wow!!!

Teamwork

In Japan, I observed that they are Master of one trade and Jack of none. A person will become perfect in his trade by years of mastering it. That's why for any project the team formation is a very common practice, so that all experts come at one place and execute the work well in time. Also, a target is assigned to a team and all team members are responsible for achieving that target. I remember one incident, when we were working on the shop floor, I observed that after the shift timing was over a group of workers did not go home but went to the machine of one worker who was still working and started to help her out. On asking it was told that the group was assigned a daily target and one worker was lagging, so without charging any overtime, the other group members pitched in so that target could be finished quickly. What a solidarity!!!

Honesty

There is no ticket checker in bus or train. In the bus near driver seat there used to be a small conveyor and while getting down you put the exact fare in the conveyor. It is by default assumed that the person will not cheat and its true. Honesty is in their blood.

Hence and therefore after a stay of 4 months in Japan, I was a changed person with completely new mental DNA

........Next chapter onwards I will describe how I implemented these learnings in my professional life.

CHAPTER SEVEN

The Test

So we were back in India and got on with installation and trial of equipment's. It turned out to be a state of art factory. The recruitment and training of the workers to produce good product was all very exhilarating.

Being an emotional person, I bring lot of passion to my work, company, and team. The veterans of industry warn against being emotional at workplace, but I disagree. Being attached to your work creates intrinsic motivation and best output. My bonding with the team was satisfactory. So much so that Union never troubled me during my stay of six and half years in that company. In fact, they used to forewarn me of any trouble brewing with management.

Learning- Be truthful to your team and work, discouraging any politics, will take you far in career.

Finally, after 2 years I became the boss of my department. And it was handful at that young age and low experience. On the way up I learnt a lot of things like.

-Loose talks can land you in trouble

-Think twice before you say anything.

-Be the master of your trade. Because people expect solutions from the boss.

- Pay utmost respect to the skill of your teammates and use it liberally to enhance quality.

-Always appreciate in public and give feedback in private.

-People will always look up to you for directions. Never ignore anyone.

Hence the outcome- there was no Quality Control section in my work area. Every operator was responsible for the good quality output from their worktables.

There was a concept of internal customer respect in department. That means every preceding Operation will treat next operation as their internal customer and pass on the product to its satisfaction. This concept was unbelievable to most of Indians.

CHAPTER EIGHT

The Shock

After spending a highly satisfying tenure of six and a half years in Japanese way of working, I decided to change. Reason- the product was becoming obsolete, and it was inevitable that factory will shut down.

Got selected in 3 companies. But I selected the one where the MD, in interview, was not ready to believe that I had no Quality department. It was a very small, owner driven, technically backward disorganised automotive Tier 1 sector.

The only reason to join was the vision of owners and the resolute determination to become one of the top companies in India. I realised that I could grow with them. The turnover was 9cr in 1993. Today it is 10000cr plus and a certified Great Place To Work. And true to my intuition, at that time, I grew from Manager Production to CEO level with the company.

The learning from above is that if you want something badly, dream for it, and are ready to work hard and smart for it, the nature opens up its arms to embrace you and reward you with bounties. Well, I experienced it first hand

On my first day of new Job my father came to drop me. He was shocked to see a three-floor dilapidated building with no approach road in a dilapidated industrial area of

Delhi. He immediately decreed that from next day I shall not come here.

So here I was with so much to do as a challenge and determined to use my capabilities learnt so far, to convert the place and here was my father worried, rightly so, about my career and future.

Anyway, I joined and remained in new company for 20 years which will be covered in subsequent chapters. By the way I was the youngest Manager in the group at that time at the age of 28.

CHAPTER NINE

The Pressure

Due to my experience in large multinationals, the expectations of management were high from day 1. Ironically, I had never worked in such a disorganised manner, so I was under pressure to perform where everything was urgent. Since the factory was set up in 1960s so we had fair number of people who were from that time and simply refused to report to me. So, things were not falling in line and I started to get frustrated and impatient with people.

The old lot refused to change and did not deviate from their outdated methods of working. Yet management was wanting to change with time. That's the reason they had hired professionals like me.

Finally, one incidence gave me the opportunity which I desperately needed. Three months into my job, there happened a breakdown in machine due to which supplies to Maruti stopped. Like other things the machine spare inventory management was also in a mess. So, the delay prolonged. Some old employees who were not happy with my methodology created a ruckus in front of Chairman. Obviously, I was called by the big boss and asked for the explanation. I took the entire blame for the fiasco without naming anyone from the team. The Chairman was speechless. He helped me to chalk out the action plan and told his son the MD to handle Maruti. Now comes the best part. He enquired about what is happening around and took two actions. First, he called the old timers and took them to task for misinforming him. Second, he called all the staff and announced that whosoever is not ready to report or support me can leave the company with immediate effect. The meeting ended at 2 AM in the night with crystal clears messages from Chairman- Change or be changed.

Learning- Be truthful and take care of your team, you will be taken care off.

From that day till his death, I was supported by chairman at all fronts. And of course, it brought changes which I wanted.

CHAPTER TEN

The Exit and Return

So, the progress went on and due to hard work of MD, more and more orders started to flow in. And with the support of the team, quality and delivery improved. But the infrastructure and machines being old, we were not able to expand in the limited space. The new sites were being explored to relocate the plants. But due to some circumstances, which I will refrain from writing, I put in my resignation. Obviously, the Chairman was upset when he came to know about it. But I requested him to let me go.

I was picked up by a company in Gurgaon which was supplying parts to Maruti. It was also owner driven but I had an excellent boss who was a thorough professional. Let's call him MKP. The factory was a gold mine of opportunities for improvement, and I was like on full blast from Day1. MKP understood this and gave me a free hand and handled the owners so that they do not interfere.

Results - The supplies to Maruti were always hand to mouth and staff of Maruti was always sitting in the factory to ensure despatches. Within 3 months we doubled the output with same number of people and the Finished goods store always had 3 days of inventory of all parts. I was thrilled because here I used all my skills learnt so far to the fullest. Naturally the management was happy. This started a campaign to look for more customers.

Learning - If you are in a position of power make efforts to create a conducive atmosphere so that each person gives his/her best. If you are not in position of power and working culture is conducive, make the best use of it, because it is a rare opportunity.

Now comes the twist in the tail. 10 months down the line the JV of the company broke up with Japanese counterparts. MKP changed the job and son of the owner took up the charge and things became bad. MKP wanted to take me with him. But without my knowing so, the Chairman of previous company took his son ,the MD to task for letting me go.

So, I got a call from MD of previous company, and he requested me to join back in another project, which has been in loss since 1993. So in last quarter of 1998 I joined back under another excellent boss. Let's call him JKM. JKM till date is a free-spirited man and kills any office politics before it starts. I was very lucky to have him as a mentor and guide. This new project was also suffering from low productivity and poor quality. So again, I was happy to face a challenge which will test my grit and skills.

CHAPTER ELEVEN

The Breakthrough

I started in new position with full vigour and a bias. Before joining, I was told that in this project the discipline is loose, and the team is not competent enough to deliver. In first six months I worked with that bias and achieved nothing because I went in with closed mind. That was my mistake. The output of factory was low, quality was a question mark, and the bottom line was continuously in red. But I found team to be excellent and competent in the desired field under a positive and very supportive leadership. So after a serious one to one talk with JKM, I changed my style of working.

Lesson Learnt - Take feedback from all but make your own assessment objectively without sentiments.

Despite all the teamwork and best efforts, the success was still elusive. We were missing something which was in plain sight, that is synchronised running of plant. We had no clue as to what to do. Seeing our predicament, MD decided to engage CII (Confederation of Indian Industries) as our consultants to guide us through. And we were introduced to the world's best management system - "Toyota Production System". After understanding the tenets of TPS, I felt like waking up from sleep. It is simple at grass root levels and addictive.

Then there was no stopping us. We immediately formed a team under my leadership and took one production line to balance and synchronise it. JKM gave me a completely free hand. It took us 6 months and the results were just amazing. The output of line went up from 700 units in 24 hours to 1200 units in 8 hours with same line and same number of operators. The key was to balance the cycle time of each process by removing "Muri - fatigue, Mura- unevenness and Muda- Wasteful activity".

Within one year we had increased the capacity of plant by 4 times, in same space with same number of people. Till that time Marketing was frustrated because the orders booked were not going out of plant on time and in quantity. Now it was my turn to demand more orders because the lines were lying idle. This made the entire marketing team and JKM to start visiting new customers and they were out 20 days in a month. That's what I call a wholistic teamwork.

Lesson - The chain is as strong as the weakest link. So, to achieve sound team work, make the weak link in your chain stronger by paying on his/her positive traits.

CHAPTER TWELVE

The Strategy - Part 1

The turnaround strategy of the plant was at two levels-Bottom Up and Top down and eventually make a companywide growth. Let me explain. This is where corporate and Japanese terms have been used, so for readers not from automotive background, I will try to explain in simple terms.

Bottom Up - There were 4 pillars for this approach. The entire work force at worker level was encouraged to engage in Small Group Activities. These were 5S, Kaizen, Quality Circles and Training. 5S is a Japanese terminology where each individual and group of individuals keep their workplaces spic and span. Only necessary items are kept on the workplace and rest are discarded. Only standard tools are used and "jugads" are removed. This results into an efficient and shining workplace with no clutter. Kaizen is a Japanese word which means "Continuous Improvement". That means each individual will do improvement in process, handling of material, removal of fatigue, balancing of flow and so on. Basically, each next day should be better than previous one in terms of working atmosphere. This is a very powerful tool for improving morale of workforce. Quality Circles are formed by 6 to 8 individuals from same department, and they take up the worst problem in the group by voting. Then through 12 step problem solving technique, they reach to the permanent solution and then take up the next problem. Imagine how robust the workplace would become by the use of these techniques. Training modules were made for generic training and specific to subject matter training. There was a classroom training and then its implementation on the workplace. Each individual was rated from 1 to 4 on the Skill Matrix chart. The aim was to take everyone to Level 3. Whosoever reached the Level 4 was made the Group Leader leading a team of 10 to 20 workers. This gave high level of optimism at worker level that they can also grow in the hierarchy of organisation.

All in all, we built a very strong foundation or what the experts call as the base of pyramid. Generally, we hire workers to use their arms and legs. Here we gave them ample platform to use their brains. You can imagine the motivation level of people at the base and a craving to perform better and better.

I will explain the TOP-Down approach in next chapter

CHAPTER THIRTEEN

The Strategy Part-2

Top-Down Strategy

In the previous chapter, the Bottom-up strategy was explained. In Top-Down Strategy, the onus was completely onto the top management. It started with setting up of "Mission" statement for the business. As it is self-explanatory the management had to set the long-term mission for the business on which the whole company would gravitate towards the final aim. For example, " To continuously enhance stakeholders value while reducing the cost and improving quality" can be one mission. It took us two days of brainstorming to reach the mission statement.

Next came the "Vision" of the organisation. The vision is more of objective statement in line with Mission statement. For example, "To increase the turnover by 3 times in 3 years and be the preferred supplier to the customer" can be the vision of organisation. We defined 2 visions for the organisation which will ultimately complete our Mission.

Next came the "Company Goals". These were the pure numbers under the headings of Q,P,C,D,S,M,E - Quality, Productivity, Cost, Delivery, Safety, Morale and Environment. The subheadings under QPCDSME had to be chosen carefully, so that when fulfilled, they lead to the achievement of Vision and Mission of the company. It was a very exciting and thrilling task, because the whole business is being institutionalised as one body. Now we had the purpose and targets and the meaning of us being there every day. These were the sacrosanct ideals and were reviewed every quarter. The ship was sailing in the right direction.

Next came the tough task of ensuring that each person is working towards the goal each hour, every day, week after week and month after month. So, we made the MP/CP (Managing Points and Control Points of each person. First the MPs were made for the top man and his CPs. The CPs of top man became the MPs of next in line and so on and so forth.

So as not to get indulged in non-value-added activity, DWM (Daily Work Management) of each staff was made. DWM is like a chronology of activities to be performed by each person each hour, each day, each week and each month.

Imagine the motivation of working in such a systematic environment. Obviously, the people attrition became minimum in the group. We used to look forward to coming to the office every morning fully charged to achieve the DWM of that day. As the time passed, we were rewarded with success which was eluding us for so long. The panic situations reduced and a relaxed way of working set in.

CHAPTER FOURTEEN

The Benchmark

Over a period, what we have done in a vertical factory, in a dilapidated industrial area became the talk of the town. Thanks to CII, delegations from other companies and delegation of CII counsellors started to visit us. It became my almost full-time job to give them the guided tour and explain the transformations.

Eventually I became the guest speaker at CII forums on Lean Manufacturing. I also became the Group champion for Lean manufacturing and the judge of Quality Circle competitions and TPS competitions within the group and outside. The plant was running on auto mode, so I became busy with visiting MBA colleges and CII forums for showcasing our journey. In the meantime, I mentored two people to become change agents. Both are doing very well in their careers.

I was told that ours is one of the 300 plants across the country who has successfully implemented Lean and that too in vertical space. We became the Benchmark for the companies in automotive sector in India. I remember an incident when a customer (gora bhai) came to visit our plant to audit and place the order. By that time, we had started lot of exports also. Gora bhai refused to enter the plant seeing the condition of the infrastructure of industrial area leave alone the audit. I remember we were standing outside on the road and trying to convince him.

Finally, he came in and after an hour he was awestruck and all ga-ga over the systematic way the raw material was going in and the assembly lines churning out parts every 9 seconds. We got the order.

Learning - If we keep crying as to what we do not have, then we shall never move forward on what we have and can do.

Eventually the plant could not take more orders, it was full to the capacity, so we decided to move to a proper industrial unit in Manesar, Gurugram. So I gaind my 4th experience of setting up a plant from scratch. By this time we were the single source to around 30 customers in India and abroad. The key was to shift the plant in such a manner that the Quality and delivery to customers was seamless.

A big thanks to my team at both the ends, that the planning was meticulous and sequential shifting started like a clockwork.

All this success eventually went to my head and as usual JKM played the balancing role of bringing me down to earth. At this point we were in discussion with an Italian giant for technical collaboration. So one more VP was hired parallel to me. We clicked so well that till today he is one of my best friends and a well-wisher. The Italian company would transfer their lines to India and start procuring from here and would shut their plant in Italy. I chose to remain with the legacy which we had created, so my friend DPM took charge of Italian part. It was so much fun working together.

In quantity we became the number 1 producer in India.

At that time Chairman took a decision to move JKM to new project which required his zeal and intelligence to turnaround that project and make a team similar to what he did with us. It was time to bring in the new CEO here. We were devastated because after working together for 10 years as a single body, our head was going to be separated from body.

CHAPTER FIFTEEN

Moving On

Everything, good or bad, finally comes to an end for greater good. So after opening another plant in Uttarakhand to cater to increasing demands and becoming Business head for both the plants and establishing ourselves as India's largest manufacturers, it was time to move on.

The best part was that we had done no recruitment from outside. All the senior positions were filled up by the people from within the organisation. Everyone grew as the business grew. With tears in the eyes and ache in the heart I bid farewell to my beloved team and moved on to another project within the group which required immediate attention of streamlining the things from purchase to delivery.

For the chairman it was a challenging task, but with what I had learnt and implemented in last so many years it was a routine task. The project was sensitive because Maruti was the customer, and they are very tough to satisfy. First task was to increase the production so that we stop working on Sundays also. Within 3 months we reached to a position where we stopped working on Saturdays and Sundays and Maruti was a happy customer. This all happened by implementing principals of Lean Manufacturing.

Now I turned my attention to team building and cost control. Within one year we were making smooth imports and handsome profit. In earlier project I had the chance to visit Japan and Indonesia to visit customers. Here I got the chance to visit my suppliers in Europe. The experience was completely opposite. I was aghast seeing the low productivity and waste of space and inventory in European countries. One CEO of our main supplier asked me jokingly, if given a chance what improvement I could do in their factory. The steps I gave sent the top management in shock. They never asked me that question again, because with their luxurious lifestyle, they did not want to change.

Learning - It is important to have one skill set in which you are master and then be the jack of rest of all.

So, the magic of previous experience worked and started to increase the customer base. One more success in my career.

Well by this time I had become the trouble shooter in the group. And wherever there was problem related to plant management, Chairman would request me to address it.

In 2010 the group decided to open a completely new non-automotive domain to enter into LED based products, Defence and Railways. The MD of domain AN was excellent choice because of his nature, his passion and especially the teamwork. I was the first choice of AN as his second in command and the domain took - off with only 3 persons onboard.

CHAPTER SIXTEEN

The Right Priority

We will go back in time, because I missed a very important situation, which forced me to re-enforce my life's priorities.

The time was April 2006, and I was at the peak of my success as a change agent and implementer of world class systems. The top team of the group was in Sariska resort, Alwar for setting up of mid-range plan for the group. That means the group was to decide where the group would be after 3 years, in terms of Business and Financial growth. Every CEO had come prepared with their plans. Since JKM was out of country, so I got the opportunity to carry the sceptre.

In the middle of the meeting, I got an overseas call from Singapore. The lady was a head-hunter and was responsible for shortlisting the Lean experts in India for a very large multinational company. She wanted my consent and kept the company name a secret. I said yes. Soon I got the confirmation that I have been short listed from India for McKinsey group (the largest consultancy group worldwide).

I was on cloud nine with just the mention of name McKinsey. I immediately bought books on McKinsey and learned about their culture. There were 3 telephonic interviews, one from China office, one from USA office and one from India office. Somehow, I sailed through. The consultant told me a figure which was four times my current salary, if I got selected. Till that time, I did not enquire about the city of placement. Finally came the moment of truth. I was sent the flight ticket to Mumbai for final round of interview with Senior Partners. I was told that a new office of Lean Manufacturing is being opened in Mumbai and I would be placed there. And would be able to come home may be once in 15 days or a month.

My whole excitement evaporated, and I went into a deep thought process, because for me my family is my first priority. I love to come home every day and have dinner with my parents, wife and kids. I had never thought of a life away from my family. My parents and wife left the decision to me. Till 12 midnight I was in a big dilemma because on one side was opportunity of lifetime to work in McKinsey with unbelievable jump in salary and a regal lifestyle, on other hand was my family, my old parents.

Finally, at 3AM in the morning, I sent regret mail to McKinsey. As expected, next day, I had to hear the earful from HR of McKinsey and my consultant for wasting everybody's time. I apologised profusely but was steadfast on my decision.

I know that some readers will feel that I was a fool to turn down life changing offer and some readers will empathise with me. But the learning is that, when I started my professional career, I had set my priorities in order of Family, Company, Salary, Designation, and till the day of my retirement, I stuck to that. Once you decide as per the set priorities in your life, you will never regret your decision. I am happy that I followed my heart and took the right decision.

CHAPTER SEVENTEEN

Out of Comfort Zone

The new domain for non-automotive products started off, with approval of project report on Solar and LED based products. This was a completely different field from the fast moving, high profile automotive division. I was totally out of my comfort zone. The gears shifted from running an established known field to un-chartered waters. In 2010 this was a new product range in India and there were no established players except for MNCs like Philips. We were given the target to be in top three position in five years. That was tough.

As we ploughed on, I realised that there is immense learning first hand, in even an unrelated field if you have the right "aptitude and attitude". So never be afraid to step out of comfort zone if you want to expand your knowledge and grow. Very soon we established the product lines and supply chain on the same principles of world class manufacturing, which I had used for so many years. That done and after handing over the divisions to respective Business Heads, I was set on the task to enter the Defence and Aerospace market.

I would admit that I was very afraid at first. But as I travelled across the country meeting defence personnel and visiting air force stations and tank manufacturing facilities, my confidence and comfort level grew. It was thrilling to sit in the cockpit of Jet fighters and know their critical operations. Finally, a detailed project report was prepared. I was surprised, as to how feasible it all looked and AN was more than pleased.

The project report was presented to the board. It was well received, but the board members were divided on the decision of taking such a big step, which had long period of return on investment. They asked for more time to deliberate on it. In the meantime, I switched over to making project report on Railway parts. I was learning something new every day.

Finally in 2014, the board took a decision that the group will not diversify away from automotive field and hence our domain would be shut down. We were all disappointed by this decision and were sure that we are losing out on a great opportunity in the new yet non-institutionalised field. That was the time when I decided to move on after having spent 20 years in one group. I also decided to follow my heart of choosing a position where I can touch and upgrade 5000 lives instead of 500 through the skills, I have acquired to wrinkle out the stresses in business processes which strain the day to day lives of so many people.

CHAPTER EIGHTEEN

A Fresh Start

With the change in mind, I started looking for the job, where I can use my skills for only improvements and no routine tasks. GOD willing, I soon landed in a Hero group company as Corporate Head of Business Excellence with a mandate to upgrade their 5 plants to world class levels (well that was too much to dream of - so I settled at making them Indian class first). It was the first time that company had established this department and I was the sole member.

I was thrilled at the opportunity and soon enough made my Blueprint for the next 3 years and presented to the management. It was accepted with a unanimous approval and pledged support of Chairman and MD. Later I came to know from Head HR that company had been trying to recruit the candidate for this position for the last 2 years and have interviewed 74 candidates before I was selected. That raised up the bar of expectation to many levels.

On this I remembered the famous lines -"Khudi ko kar buland itna ke har takdeer se pehle khuda bande se khud puche bata teri raza kya hai".

Now the biggest challenge was that none of the plants were reporting to me, yet I have to get the work done there without creating dis-harmony. The first thing to do was to make presentations to all plants and sell my ideas to their advantage so that I have a complete buy-in. Second was not to pull my rank, but work with all levels as their partner. Third at no cost negative feedback to be given to management. This is called **"Servant Leadership"**.

Within three months I established my credibility in all the plants on following counts:

1. Sincerity in upgrading the plants by working along with them and not against them.

2. I am not a management man, but a true blue, white collar and blue collar person as per the need.

3. Whatever be the case, I will never speak against the plants in reviews and open forums.

So, I quickly became one of them instead of corporate stooge and they used to look forward to my visits and new inputs. 50% of the task was done. Then I turned my attention to making an Excellence Manual for the company, consisting of all procedures, policies, formats and work instructions drawn from best of the companies in India. It took us 15 months to compile the manual and implement its first phase.

Chairman was thrilled and formally launched it digitally and made it mandatory for plants to include its compliance status in their MIS review once a month. One day he called me and told me that what I have done has made the task easier for next generations because now the company is running on set norms instead of whims and fancies of bosses.

Another learning was that the conviction of your thoughts and actions should be so deep, that it becomes contagious.

Next, we set up the basic five pillars of excellence and started driving the plants in that direction. At one time I was travelling as high as 19 days in a month and was thoroughly enjoying it. The satisfaction level was at its pinnacle. Then one day out of concern my MD told me to reduce the visits, so that I can have more dinners with my family. It was a great place to work.

Achieving the Pinnacle

Due to hard work put in by all Plants, after 2 years, we were in a state where the plants were proud to show it off to customers, visitors, and Management. But remember there is always scope for continuous improvement. The excellence journey continued.

We had reached a point where we started thinking of getting Global awards. We selected the tough and prestigious TPM (Total Productive Maintenance) award given by JIPM (Japan Institute of Plant Maintenance). To get this award, the teams must work relentlessly for 3 years to be ready for the auditors from JIPM. Globally this award is given to a Plant which has nursed their plant back to its mint state and increased the longevity of their equipment. There are very few companies in India who have qualified for this award. We selected our biggest plant in Haridwar for this award.

The Plant Head AS was a dynamic leader and excellent team player. He was totally committed to get this award. Since we vibrated on same frequency, it made my task much easier. We hired a Japanese consultant to guide us through this journey. It was invigorating and brand-new learning experience. Through passion and rigours of team and about 14 mock audits by me we were ready for JIPM audit in 2 years' time.

Finally in June 2016, the D-Day arrived and we had 2 days of strenuous audit by JIPM auditors. It was a preparatory audit. They gave us some non-conformities. The Final audit took place in December 2016, and we got our name in the list of TPM award winners by JIPM along with other companies world-wide. In March 2017, a team went to Tokyo to receive the award.

I say we achieved the peak of excellence and pride with this award. This encouraged us to repeat the experience in 3 other plants as well.

Learning – There is no short cut to hard work.

The 2nd Inning

Soon I started to get restless and was wanting to do something else, like be on my own after reaching the pinnacle. But everyone suggested that it is not the right time yet. So, I left the company in September 2017 and joined a transformer manufacturing company as Director Operations overlooking 8 plants.

It was a completely disorganised sector, and I was again in a state of challenge to rectify the situation. The Quality rejection was as high as 20% and productivity very low. Again, the same principles were applied, and Quality rejection was brought down to 0.5%. Productivity went up by 50%. Having done that in 9 months' time, I started to look for new challenge. I was not at all interested in routine mundane job.

Since I treated this period as gestation and learning period in different sectors before I strike out on my own, so yet again I made a change to Helmet manufacturing company which was in losses for the last 3 years. Another challenge worth taking on. In 6 months', time period, the company was turned into a profitable unit.

Then in January 2019, I became a free lance consultant. I took up assignments in varied sectors like pharmaceutical, renewable energy, automotive to name a few. Then the

Corona started its devastation on world, and I was out of work. Fortunately, one of the companies where I was working as consultant hired me as Corporate Quality Head. After spending 18 months there, I got retired on 1st July 2021. And guess what at my retirement my chairman was none other than my mentor JKM who had joined the same company 4 months back. What a privilege and good sign of fortune it was. My 2nd inning started on that day.

Currently I am again doing Consultancy work and enjoying my life thoroughly. I am my own boss with no tensions of office, customers, or bosses. I am taking life at a leisurely pace, spending more time with my wife, myself, my pet and my kids (whenever they are in India). I never realised that life would be as beautiful and bountiful as in 1st inning.

Learning – There is time to work hard, time to chase your passion, time to give back to society and time to sit back and enjoy. Everything should be done at the right time, and you will have no regrets in life.

The Only Constant Is Change

Dear readers, that has been My Life so far, may be we meet again with my experiences of 2nd innings